Glastonbury

Written by

Michael Mathias

Photographs by

Derek Hector

David & Charles
Newton Abbot   London   North Pomfret (Vt)

British Library Cataloguing in Publication Data

Mathias, Michael
   Glastonbury.
   1. Glastonbury, Eng.—History
   I. Title II. Hector, Derek
   942.3'83   DA690.G45
   ISBN 0-7153-7798-1

Library of Congress Catalog Card Number 79-51083

Typeset by ABM Typographics Limited, Hull
and printed in Great Britain
by Redwood Burn Limited, Trowbridge
for David & Charles (Publishers) Limited
Brunel House Newton Abbot   Devon

Published in the United States of America
by David & Charles Inc
North Pomfret   Vermont 05053   USA

CONTENTS

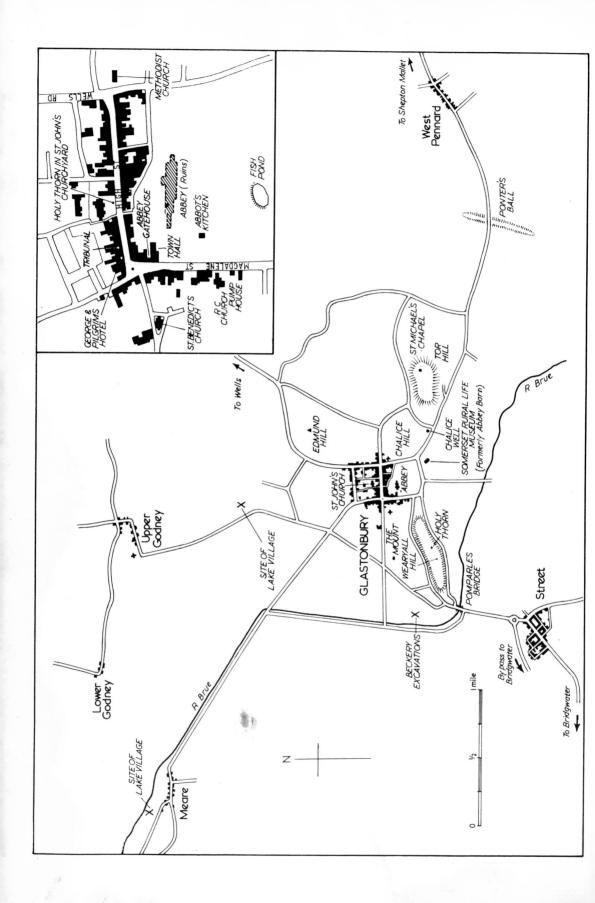

INTRODUCTION

Tourists at Glastonbury become pilgrims, visiting for the experience rather than mere visual appreciation.

Surrounded by moors, Glastonbury today is a 7,000-population market town with an exceptional past based on the former Abbey, attractively set in a 40-acre site around which the centre of the town has been built.

Before Oxford and Cambridge Universities had been founded, Glastonbury was the main seat of learning in southern England. It was a foundation of immense wealth, second only to Westminster Abbey, and a vast landowner. Henry VIII left it until the end of the line in his sacking of the monastries at the Dissolution, such was Glastonbury's influence and importance.

The Abbey gained this status in its own right, but behind this were claims that set it apart from all other religious centres in the country, even the world. These claims are ascribed to legend, and proving them is beyond the wit of man at the present time.

According to medieval traditions, Glastonbury was visited by Christ as a boy with his uncle, Joseph of Arimathea, who, only a few years after the Crucifixion, returned with the Christian gospel, to preach it first at Glastonbury. On his arrival, Joseph apparently put his wooden staff into the ground and it immediately took root and became as a young live tree. It is now immortalised as the Holy Thorn with the special attribute of blossoming twice a year, in the spring and at Christmas, when sprays are sent each year to the Queen and the Queen Mother.

Joseph is said to have brought the Chalice of the Last Supper with him plus two cruets containing the blood and sweat of Christ. Glastonbury's legends also connect the Abbey with the patron saint of Wales (David) and Ireland (Patrick). The King of Legends, Arthur, the last of the great British warriors, is said to have been buried in the Abbey.

Glastonbury was apparently a religious centre long before Christianity. The Druids possibly made use of the island sanctuary, and about 2,700 BC ancient astronomer-priests are believed to have laid out a twelve-sign zodiac with all the normal constellations physically mapped out on the ground in the correct sequence within a ten-mile radius.

This is but a foretaste of the unique claims that account for Glastonbury's worldwide attraction, now experienced by hundreds of thousands of people each year.

The magnificent tower of St John's Church is currently being restored. The present church was built on Norman foundations between 1400 and 1500; the tower dates from 1475. The Holy Thorn is seen in front of the Church. A thirteenth-century crucifix and a brass alms dish that once belonged to the Abbey are among the Church's treasures. Others include some fifteenth-century furniture and stained glass and an altar tomb of the same period. There are also some paintings and copies of old masters, a fifteenth-century Italian marble relief of the Nativity and early churchwardens' accounts and records from the fourteenth century onwards.

5

Mist shrouds Glastonbury Tor. An engaging and perceptive description of this feature of the Glastonbury landscape was given to the Somerset Archaeological and Natural History Society by Mr A. Fownes Somerville in his June 1907 presidential address, a few days after the sale of the Abbey:

The early legends and poetic traditions, which hover around those grey old ruins, are like the November mists and fogs which sweep silently over the moorlands up to the Isle of Avalon, blotting out the landscape, save here and there, leaving us in a world of ghostly mystery. We know that below is the firm soil, and that the white-winged spectres, which our fancy created out of the curling mists, will fade away when the sun bursts forth again, and that the sudden landscape will reappear.

The stern historian analyses and discards the tradition and legendary lore; he cannot see below them; for him there is no sun except the light of documentary evidence. But most of us have an innate, it may be childlike, faith in that hidden landscape, and we shall continue to believe, in spite of our stern historian's warnings and rebukes, that in Glastonbury we have a link with the earliest history of the British church of today . . .

(*Aerial photograph by West Air Photography*)

Christmas blossom from the Holy Thorn being cut for the Queen and Queen Mother, a custom said to have started in the time of Queen Anne. It lapsed and was revived during the reign of King George V and continued, apart from one year; that year a letter was received saying how much the late Queen Mary had missed the spray. The spray of blossom is put on the Royal breakfast table on Christmas Day. It is a Glastonbury custom that the blossom is cut by the Mayor in St John's churchyard. The tree in the picture was planted in 1900 and there is another in the same churchyard. Several others thrive in the town, including private gardens and the Abbey grounds. A Glastonbury nurseryman who used to propagate the trees said that this was done by grafting onto a blackthorn in a similar way to budding a rose.

Holy Thorn trees have been sent all over the world, including New York's Central Park, Washington Cathedral, Toronto and many places in continental Europe. A spray was sent to America for President John Kennedy's funeral.

Stones laid bare by man and time. The scene beside the
north wall of the Lady Chapel of Glastonbury Abbey.

1
THE EARLIEST GLASTONIANS

Seven main areas in and around Glastonbury have been scientifically excavated by archaeologists in the hope of finding proof of the early legendary Christian settlements. The proof has not been there. Yet this has done nothing to diminish interest in these legends.

In prehistoric times Glastonbury was an 'island', isolated in the centre of near sea-level marshes. These stretch north fourteen miles to the Bristol Channel, east to the Mendip hills and west to the low-lying Polden hills.

Legends aside, the earliest visiting cards left by man on this landscape were trackways, far out on the marshes, and a number of Mesolithic flints found beside Glastonbury's Chalice Spring. These were not enough to indicate a settlement, but rather people making use of a good water supply.

By some strange twist of fate there is at the moment no proof of actual human occupation, other than frequentation, in Glastonbury until the fifth and sixth centuries AD. Logically it is absurd that these few hills enjoying isolation, excellent views and an abundant water supply should be ignored by prehistoric and early Christian people. Only a mile away there is abundant evidence of occupation for some 250 years of this 'missing' period by people who lived in what is termed a 'lake village' on the swampy moor. There was another lake village two miles away at Meare and, thanks to the preservative nature of the peat bog upon which they built their homes, a great deal is known about them. They, at least, were certainly not isolated. Finds have included items originating from Dorset, Cornwall, Yorkshire and the Baltic.

Then, some time during the first century AD, maybe because of a change in the conditions of dryness on the moors or through external conquest, the villages were abandoned. The people vanished. To add to the enigma these people have no known burial ground for that 250-year occupation.

The historical blackout ends in the post-Roman Dark Ages with a confirmed sixth-century occupation on the Tor by people of some importance for those days, shown by the remains of imported wine jars and metalwork practised on the 520ft summit. Archaeologist Philip Rahtz, who excavated the summit area for three seasons, now believes this was most likely a monastic settlement.

The Abbey site may well have had an earlier occupation than the Tor, but all that can be said with absolute certainty is that there was a monastic settlement on the present site by the third quarter of the seventh century.

It is thought there might have been a Roman villa in Glastonbury—possibly in the area of the present High Street. Support for this theory comes from the fragments of Romano-British pottery found on the Abbey site. These were in layers of clay imported in the thirteenth century to level up the floors of the church and cloisters. The soil must have come from close by, and if that spot could be found, doubtless some of the secrets of Glastonbury's missing period could be revealed.

Despite all the magnificence and seemingly unchallenged certainty of the legends and traditions, proving them is like trying to capture the wind—you can feel its force, but never hold it in your hands. Believers court exposure to the force of the legends, sometimes esoterically, thereby transforming Glastonbury into a cult.

Scholars and scientists have done their best with their professional skills and reputations for almost a century, and neither sustained nor damaged the standing of the traditions.

2
THE LEGENDS

It is important to realise that the written accounts of the Glastonbury legends are only half as old as the events they describe.

Joseph of Arimathea, Arthur and St David were first chronicled by medieval writers, hundreds of years after they had died. Pre-Norman Conquest writers neither mention them not a host of other details that place Glastonbury in its exclusive position. And, sadly, even the first medieval documents have suffered through later editing and additions that have been embellished, confusing the historical original. This does not mean the documents have lost all credulity, but they have to be treated with as much caution as respect.

Joseph of Arimathea

Simplified to their essentials, the legends say that as a boy Jesus visited Glastonbury with his uncle Joseph of Arimathea, a tin trader, who came to the Westcountry for Cornish tin and Mendip lead. This particular visit is said to have been the inspiration for William Blake's hymn 'Jerusalem' which begins:

> And did those feet in ancient time
> Walk upon England's mountains green?

Joseph, who took Christ's body down from the cross and placed it in his sepulchre, is said to have returned to Britain some years later—AD 37 or 63—bringing the Christian message. With eleven companions, or disciples, he made his way to Glastonbury to be among the friendly and influential Druids he had known from the past. When, on arrival, he put his wooden staff into the ground with such a miraculous result, this was a divine sign that he had come to his journey's end.

The Chalice Cup

The Chalice Cup of the Last Supper which Joseph is said to have brought with him has become entangled in myth and is identified as the cup of plenty or the Holy Grail of Arthurian fame. The cruets containing the blood and sweat of Christ were said to have been buried with Joseph in his Glastonbury grave.

The Old Church

The local ruler, King Arviragus, gave Joseph and his party twelve hides of land in and around Glastonbury, and on part of it the group built the wattle and daub church, dedicated to the Virgin Mary. Its traditional site is where the Abbey's Lady Chapel was later built. It had the

The Holy Thorn in flower. As well as blossoming twice a year, the tree can sometimes show evidence of the four seasons at the same time: bud, blossom, berry and dead leaf. The Puritan fanatic who cut down the reputed original planted by Joseph of Arimathea is said to have been blinded by a flying splint for his trouble; he failed to completely sever the trunk, thus enabling resuscitation to take place.

Glastonbury Abbey. The steps on the other side of the railings led up to the west door of the Great Church. In front of the steps is the Galilee, forming a porch or vestibule. The photograph has been taken from a wooden bridge spanning the crypt under the Lady Chapel, or St Joseph's Chapel as it is also known. The crypt was an early sixteenth century addition of Abbot Bere who encouraged the cult of St Joseph. This is the traditional site of the *Vetusta Ecclesia* or Old Church attributed to Joseph of Arimathea and dedicated to the Virgin Mary. It is certain that a wattle and daub church of great antiquity was preserved for centuries in this spot, until the shrine was destroyed in the 1184 fire. The Lady Chapel was the first part of the Abbey built after the fire.

name *Vetusta Ecclesia*, or Old Church and, though dilapidated in later centuries, did not finally disappear until a tragic fire swept the Abbey in 1184.

The Establishment of the Abbey

In the next century, the legends continue, Pope Elutherius, at the request of Arviragus's grandson, King Lucius, sent two missionaries, Deruvian and Phagan, to invigorate the work at Glastonbury. The two are credited with first establishing the Abbey, but other accounts say it was founded in the fifth century by St Patrick who was abbot before leading the conversion of Ireland. St David of Wales is reputed to have travelled to Glastonbury at a later date with seven bishops to dedicate the Old Church, but he was warned in a dream that the Lord himself had already done so. Instead, David added another church and dedicated that.

Arthur

Arthur, the great warrior, more naturally belongs to his Camelot, across the moors at South Cadbury, and excavations in the late '60s have adequately confirmed superb fortifications there during Arthur's fifth-century lifetime. But

Pomparles Bridge on the main road between Glastonbury and Street with the River Brue flowing underneath. This is the bridge from which Arthur's sword Excalibur is said to have been thrown into the waters of the Brue. But the Arthurian link does not seem to have been acknowledged in the bridge's name until 1344, when it was called *pontem periculosam* or the Pons Perilis of Arthurian legend.

Arthur's dead body certainly belongs to Glastonbury. Following the fateful battle of Camlann, the wounded Arthur was brought to the Isle of Avalon, the isle of the dead which is identified as Glastonbury, for burial. In 1191 monks at Glastonbury claimed to have found his remains just south of the Lady Chapel, and King Edward I and Queen Matilda witnessed their reburial in front of the Abbey's high altar in 1278.

Legend also tells us that Arthur parted with his famous sword Excalibur at Glastonbury. As he threw it from the Pomparles Bridge, on the main road between Glastonbury and Street, a a hand appeared from the waters of the River Brue to take it into safe custody.

Another tale links him with the little chapel on the island of Beckery—now next door to the town's sewage works. Arthur had been told by an angel to go there and when he did so saw Mary with the infant Jesus.

The Holy Grail quest, if equated with a search for the Chalice of the Last Supper brought over by Joseph of Arimathea, would have involved Arthur at Glastonbury; one supposed hiding place of the Chalice was at the bottom of the well of that name. But it is an unlikely story because the name 'Chalice Well' was another medieval transplant. It was not a local name until after 1306, and the alternative name of 'blood spring' comes from the iron in the water which leaves an iron-red deposit on the stones over which it passes. Arthur has also been linked with the mythology of the Glastonbury Zodiac, being identified as the sign Sagittarius, and the Zodiac has been regarded as the 'round table'.

3
THE ARCHAEOLOGISTS' FINDINGS

The popular belief that in ancient times Glastonbury was an island surrounded by water or impenetrable marshes is false. Archaeologist Philip Rahtz calls it unthinkable. The water level was never permanently high enough to completely cut off Glastonbury from the mainland, according to pollen analyses and radiocarbon investigations of prehistoric conditions on the moor. Had the water level been high enough to surround Glastonbury, the lake villages at Meare and Glastonbury would have been awash.

Iron Age Lake Villages

The inhabitants of these Iron Age villages in the marshes sealed their homes from the damp underneath by importing clay for their floors, which were regularly topped up. Those at the Glastonbury village would have either gone to Godney or Glastonbury 'island' for their clay, both more than half-a-mile from their homes.

An idea of the vast quantity of earth involved comes from one Glastonbury dwelling mound, which had about 150 tons of clay on the floor—and there were 60-70 huts in the village.

Arthur Bulleid, who discovered the village and led the excavations, said that every scrap of clay, gravel, stone and doubtless a large proportion of the timber had to be imported. The rubble came from the foot of the Tor about a mile away. Other stones were traced to the Mendips, about six miles distant. Yet these people preferred to live on the moors for about 250 years in circular wooden huts surrounded by their defensive palisades rather than on the nearby dry land.

Among the finds were some brooches of safety-

The Abbot's Fish House at Meare, three miles from the Abbey, was built in the early fourteenth century on the banks of Meare Pool, a vital source of fish supplies for the Abbey. The house was the home of the head fisherman, who lived on the upper floor and kept the tackle and cured fish on the ground floor. The pool was stocked with pike, roach, tench, eels and there were many swans. The greatest call on the skills of the fisherman and his staff was during lent, when meat was forbidden.

The bronze Glastonbury Bowl.

A chronological list of Glastonbury's abbots spanning almost 1,000 years. Aegelnoth, at the bottom of the first column, was the last of the Saxon abbots. He had to live through the changes resulting from the Norman Conquest, ending, for him, in the trauma of being thrown out by armed Norman knights. His successor, Thurstin or Turstin, did not see Christian eye to eye with the Saxon monks who remained, and in one quarrel he had archers brought into the church to shoot the troublesome members of the community.

Since the Dissolution, the Roman Catholic Church has occasionally used the title of Abbot of Glastonbury. This has been more or less continuously held by a Benedictine monk since 1820. The present Abbot of Glastonbury is Dom Aelred Watkin, aged 60 in 1979, a former headmaster of Downside School. The title does not pass from him until he dies.

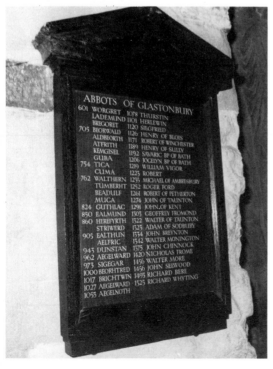

pin design that match those of another lake village people—in Switzerland. They were also a Celtic tribe, living at La Tène, a military station near Neuchâtel. About forty-five brooches of the 'La Tène' period were discovered at the Glastonbury lake village.

Most famous of the lake village finds was the Glastonbury Bowl, a circular bronze bowl made in two sections and joined together by rivets with rounded heads. It measured four-and-a-half inches deep. The rim was ornamented with two finely-waved lines.

The Swiss lake villages passed into oblivion at the hands of the Romans. Those at Glastonbury and Meare are believed to have ended with a massacre some time before the Roman conquest of Britain. The few human remains, just 49, found at Glastonbury, show evidence of violent butchery, some being decapitated and others having their bodies hacked to pieces. Whatever the purpose of the attack, it imposed a void in the historical time-scale that has only been filled by legend. It is tantalising to think that if the villages were not sacked until AD 50, its inhabitants were living their domesticated late Iron Age lives when Christ may have visited Glastonbury and when Joseph of Arimathea returned with the gospel.

Glastonbury Abbey

Light at the end of the tunnel only begins to emerge well into the post-Roman Dark Ages. Dr C. A. Ralegh Radford, who was director of excavations at the Abbey for many years, says the earliest known remains are a cemetary, an enclosure called the 'great bank' and wattled timber oratories. These can be specifically dated to the seventh century. H. P. R. Finberg, Professor of English Local History at Leicester University, has said that there is no convincing evidence, either documentary or archaeological, for the existence of a monastic institution at Glastonbury before the third quarter of the seventh century.

Stories still persist that St Patrick, who died about 461 AD, was associated with Glastonbury. William of Malmesbury, an authoritative post-Conquest historian and monk, attributed the real beginnings of Glastonbury to him. Patrick's tomb was said to be beside the altar of the Old Church. A chapel dedicated to St Patrick is in use now, but dates from the early sixteenth century. William's works have been enhanced by other writers, but of the early medieval historians to write on Glastonbury, he is the one

taken most seriously. He was invited to write about the antiquity of Glastonbury between 1125 and 1130, and had use of the Abbey's library and records, but modern historians believe even he may have been over-generous in some of his assertions, influenced by a desire not to offend his hosts.

When the Saxons arrived as far west as Glastonbury, called Ynys-witrin before their arrival, they had been converted to Christianity, so the Abbey building was not adversely interfered with, an unpleasant habit of their pre-Christian past.

The man who had done most to prevent typical Saxon vandalism lay buried beneath their feet. He was Arthur, hero of the Battle of Badon which halted the Saxon advance. This victory brought peace for about sixty years, long enough for the crucial Christianisation of the Saxons. Desecration now gave way to devotion.

The Saxon King of Wessex, Ine, gave the Abbey fresh momentum in the first years of the eighth century by building a new church to the east of the wattle Old Church of ancient and perhaps divine origin. Under the Saxons Glastonbury became an important institution as seen by the burial of Edward the Elder, Edgar the Peacemaker and Edmund Ironside, three of their kings, at the Abbey.

The Abbot's Kitchen, dating from the fourteenth century, is the only monastic structure still intact. It has a vaulted dome and four large chimneys in the inside corners. That the abbot had such a vast kitchen was a sign of the wealth of the Abbey. It formed part of the rebuilding of the Abbot's House by Abbot Breynton.

By far the most important Saxon abbot was Dunstan. Born a few miles away at Baltonsborough, the son of a West Saxon noble, he became abbot about 943. His main achievement at Glastonbury was his reform of monastic life according to the strict Benedictine rule, and under his abbacy Glastonbury became a famous school. His reforming zeal spread to other Benedictine foundations and his diplomatic and statesmanlike attributes were called into use by the kings under whom he served. He later became Archbishop of Canterbury. At the time of the Domesday survey in 1087 the Abbey's possessions spread over most of the surrounding moors and the Polden hills and included thirteen watermills.

The 1184 Fire and Arthur's Grave
An unfortunate milestone in the Abbey's history was the fire of 1184 which burnt down the Old Church and the enormous Norman church of Abbot Herlewin, and destroyed the records and

15

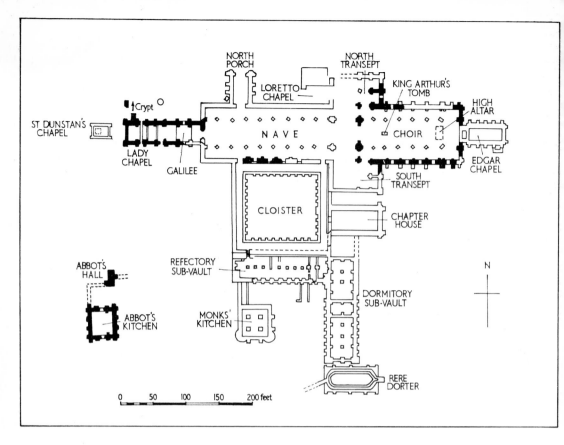

A plan of Glastonbury Abbey; see also the scale model on page 39.

library that William of Malmesbury had had the good fortune to inspect sixty years before.

Seven years after the fire, the monks claimed to have discovered the graves of Arthur and Guinevere south of the Lady Chapel wall. Their relics were said to be sixteen feet down in the hollowed-out trunk of an oak tree. With them was a leaden cross with the Latin inscription: 'Here lies Arthur, the famous king of the Isle of Avalon'. Against the political and domestic background of the time, the monks could have made an extremely convenient discovery: Henry II was having problems with the Welsh, who believed that Arthur was sleeping and would return one day and lead them to victory. To prove Arthur was dead by finding his grave made political sense.

Also, after 600 years of silence, the forgotten warrior was becoming a cult hero. By finding his grave, the additional kudos for the Abbey would bring in more pilgrims to make contributions towards the large sums of money needed for the rebuilding.

Excavating at the same spot, archaeologists found a break in the charred earth resulting from the fire, and the base of a pyramid said to be

The site of King Arthur's tomb. The inscription reads: 'In the year 1191 the bodies of King Arthur and his queen were said to have been found on the south side of the Lady Chapel. On 19th April 1278 their remains were removed in the presence of King Edward I and Queen Eleanor to a black marble tomb on this site. This tomb survived until the Dissolution of the Abbey in 1539.' The tomb was enshrined in the centre of the choir. The base of it was discovered in 1934.

Abbots of Glastonbury in the Middle Ages had a judicial franchise over a wide area in and around Glastonbury known as the Twelve Hides. It was from this Tribunal building in the High Street that justice over this area was administered, in the name of the abbot. The present building originated some time after 1400, but the court records tell of trials at a County Hall at Glastonbury in the thirteenth century. This earlier building probably stood on the same site. The present stone facade was constructed by Abbot Bere (1493-1524) to give light to the courtroom on the front of the upper floor. Since the Dissolution the building has been used as a dwelling and a school and is now administered by the Department of the Environment. The museum of the Glastonbury Antiquarian Society is housed on the upper floor and is concerned mainly with the lake village finds, including the Glastonbury Bowl of bronze and a dugout canoe.

SITE OF KING ARTHUR'S TOMB.
IN THE YEAR 1191 THE BODIES OF
KING ARTHUR AND HIS QUEEN WERE
SAID TO HAVE BEEN FOUND ON THE
SOUTH SIDE OF THE LADY CHAPEL.
ON 19TH APRIL 1278 THEIR REMAINS WERE
REMOVED IN THE PRESENCE OF
KING EDWARD I AND QUEEN ELEANOR
TO A BLACK MARBLE TOMB ON THIS SITE.
THIS TOMB SURVIVED UNTIL THE
DISSOLUTION OF THE ABBEY IN 1539.

next to the graves. This, at least, confirms part of the monks' story.

In 1278 King Edward I was present at the Abbey for the reburial of Arthur's bones in a black marble tomb in front of the Abbey's high altar. This tomb survived until the Dissolution in 1539 and its site was rediscovered during excavations in 1934. It is now clearly marked in the ruins.

The last of the great building abbots, Abbot Bere, developed a Joseph of Arimathea cult and built a crypt dedicated to him under the Lady Chapel. He also added the Loretto Chapel and may have started the Edgar Chapel, finished by Abbot Whyting, the former following a visit to Rome and the latter as a shrine for the three Saxon kings. He rebuilt St Benedict's Church, finished off St John's Church and built the Tribunal as a courthouse for hearing cases inside the Abbey's area of jurisdiction—within the twelve hides.

The Sacking of the Abbey

The Abbey only survived another fourteen years after Abbot Bere's death before it was seized by Henry VIII's men and sacked.

At the time of the Dissolution in 1539, the Abbey had 100 monks. Abbot Richard Whyting, who was 'upwards of 90 years', kept and maintained 300 domestics who lived in the town and supported many students in university. Glaston-

This gives an idea of the size and ravaged beauty of the Abbey. In the foregorund is the site of the Edgar Chapel; then into the choir with the high altar and Arthur's tomb marked out on the ground. On the other side of the piers which once supported the central tower are the nave and west doorway. In the distance is one of the turrets of the Lady Chapel.

The original Abbey buildings were constructed of lias stone from Keinton Mandeville, about seven miles away. After the 1184 fire the monks rebuilt with Doulting stone, a hard Mendip limestone still quarried in large quantities today.

Looking across the old vault under the monk's refectory and the grassed-over cloisters to the south walls of the nave of the Great Church and, lower down, the Lady Chapel. It was in front of this southern wall of the Lady Chapel that the monks found what they claimed to be the remains of King Arthur and Queen Guinevere in 1191.

(below)
A view across the choir with the tower of St John's Church in the background. (*Brian Walker*)

The richly ornamented Romanesque south door into the Lady Chapel.

bury was among the last few monasteries in the country to be supressed.

The final drama began at the abbot's Sharpham Manor. Henry's men demanded Whyting surrender the Abbey. He refused. A search was made, and in Whyting's study a book against the king's divorce was discovered; some say it had been planted. Whyting was indicted, tried and found guilty of high treason. The sentence: execution. It was a gruesome one. Whyting was dragged on a hurdle from Wells through the town to the top of the Tor where he was hanged, still wearing his monk's habit. His body was then beheaded and quartered, the head being reserved as a spectacle at the Abbey's main gate, and the quarters being distributed for public attention to Bath, Wells, Ilchester and Taunton.

Also killed with Whyting on the Tor were his treasurer, John Thorn, and under-treasurer, Roger James, both monks. The revenue from the Abbey and its estates at the Dissolution was initially assessed at £3,311 7s 4½d per annum. A more detailed valuation raised the total to £3,508 13s 4¾d—just about the same wealth as Westminster Abbey.

The first owner of the Abbey after the Dissolution was Edward Seymour, Duke of Somerset, but until it passed into the hands of the Church of England in 1907 there were several owners. Ownership at one stage was gained at a game of dice. Much of the Abbey's missing masonry was sold by past owners for houses and road-building. Gunpowder had to be used to break up some of the walls; the mortar was so strong it was hard to break a stone clean of it. According to later writers, those who used the stone for homes or other buildings did not thrive, nor did the buildings stand long. The town's market house suffered a collapse in the seventeenth century, attributed by townspeople to the fact that the large new building was constructed by William Strode Esq, out of stone from a large vault in the Abbey ruins.

Glastonbury Tor

The Abbey had two satellite monastic settlements in Glastonbury, on the summit of the Tor and at Beckery.

From the Tor's earliest known period of settlement, in the Dark Ages when Arthur's Camelot fort twelve miles away on the southern horizon was still operational, has come a still unexplained discovery. At first sight it appeared to be a grave with a big stone built over

This vault was built under the Galilee about 1320 to form a link with the Great Church. The altar is used during services held in the Lady Chapel crypt.

St Michael's tower on the 520ft summit of Glastonbury Tor. This is all that remains of the medieval church built to replace an earlier one destroyed by a landslide or 'earthquake' in 1275.

There is a strong belief in a cave inside the Tor. Tor maze theorist Geoffrey Russell, the late Chosen Chief of the Order of Bards, Ovates and Druids, Ross Nichols, and the late Wellesley Tudor Pole, former chairman of the Chalice Well Trust, were just three subscribing to this belief. During the excavations between 1964-66 archaeologist Philip Rahtz said he would have loved to have found one. He once thought the fissures on the summit might give access to a cave, but found no evidence.

it. Large and small blocks of stone, some burnt red and all looking as if they had been deliberately placed, gave archaeologist Philip Rahtz, director of excavations, and his helpers high expectation of finding something rare.

The stones were carefully removed, but the mystery remained. Underneath, in a shallow hollow, were an iron ferrule, a patch of wood-ash and evidence of a small fissure in the rock. It was even impossible to tell if the hollow was natural or had been dug away. A Dark Age grave in that position would most certainly have been a rich one, with some treasure. The cairn, as it is officially known, was about twelve feet long by five feet at its widest point, and on a north to south alignment.

Philip Rahtz thought it might even have been commemorating someone who had died but whose body had been lost. The late Major Wellesley Tudor Pole, chairman of the Chalice Well Trust which sponsored the excavation, and a man of great psychic and spiritual insight, believed some quite important discovery was being 'held back'. It was nothing to worry about, he said; room must be left for future generations to make further finds.

Evidence of monastic cells and possibly a wooden church on the Tor during the pre-Conquest period were also unearthed. A later stone church, dedicated to St Michael, was flattened by a severe 'earthquake' or landslide on 11 September, 1275. It was replaced; but all that now remains is the imposing tower that dominates the Glastonbury landscape. Every year it draws thousands of pilgrims to share its airy prominence over the Vale of Avalon. The tower is a symbol hundreds of millions of people all over the world have carried with them at some time in their lives during the past 150 years. Clarks, the shoe manufacturers whose headquarters faces the Tor from neighbouring Street, use it as their trademark. The image of St Michael's tower stamped on millions of shoes, is a fitting symbol for pilgrims.

The Beckery Monastic Settlement

The Beckery settlement was also famed for its pilgrims. The name means 'Little Ireland' and, according to legend, the Irish St Bridget lived here for a time in the late fifth century. On her return to Ireland she left behind some of her possessions—a bag, wallet, necklace and bell—which were displayed and adored. And St Patrick, having been Glastonbury's abbot, was another reason to attract the Irish. Beckery was

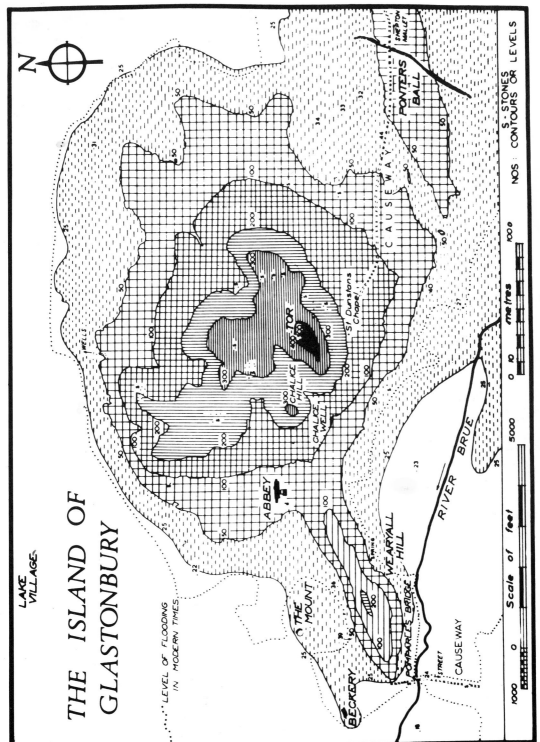

Topographical map of Glastonbury Tor

the first landfall for travellers using the River Brue waterway into Glastonbury from the west and it was for a time said to have been 'colonised' by the visiting Irish.

Excavations during 1887 at Beckery produced enough to justify further probing for proof of the elusive fifth-century Christian activity. These were carried out in 1967 and 1968, under the direction of Philip Rahtz and Susan Hirst, again under the main sponsorship of the Chalice Well Trust. The earliest finds followed a familiar pattern: prehistoric flints, a few shards of lake village and Roman pottery— all adding up to evidence of visits by people living in these times, but no settlement.

Absence of pottery imported from the eastern Mediterranean probably meant that the first settlement, which included a chapel, was not before the seventh century. A cemetery of the same period was found and sixty-three graves excavated. Samples of bone from forty-eight individuals were submitted for radiocarbon analysis and given a date of about 730 AD. Only three of them were not adult males. These com-

prised two juveniles and a woman; she was not buried in any significant position, so was more likely a domestic servant than St Bridget. A second chapel, which could have been built before the Conquest, was found and this was replaced by a third, built during the second half of the thirteenth-century.

The Mount and Ponter's Ball

Two other sites excavated in Glastonbury, The Mount, near Beckery, and Ponter's Ball may possibly be inter-related. Ponter's Ball is a low embankment straddling the eastern approaches

The Abbey Barn was used to store farm produce for 600 years, from the days of the Abbey until 1972 when the farm owner gave the Barn to Somerset County Council to be used as a rural life museum. It opened in its new role in August 1977. Among the exhibits is a collection of farm carts and wagons from Somerset including one from the former Abbey Farm, horse-drawn agricultural machinery, boats from the Somerset levels, cider-making equipment used in Glastonbury in the 1880s and a farmhouse kitchen display reflecting the life story of John Hodges, a Victorian farm labourer from the neighbouring village of Butleigh.

to Glastonbury from the Pilton and Shepton Mallet direction. It rises to a height of twenty-one feet, is about thirty feet across and is more than half-a-mile long.

The theory that it was a demarkation line between secular and sacred worlds was gently rocked when excavations in 1970 revealed twelfth-century pottery under the Iron Age levels. What makes the theory of medieval construction plausible is that it may be linked with the motte and bailey fort built by Henry of Blois, abbot from 1126 to 1171, at The Mount, between Beckery and Wearyall Hill. Henry, William the Conqueror's grandson and King Stephen's brother, had switched sides in a civil war, and he may have feared reprisals. The fort was possibly part of an early warning system if raiders approached via the river Brue. He could have built Ponter's Ball with the same intention. It would have given sufficient advance warning of hostile movement from the east. On the approach from Wells there was another embankment, called Fountain's Wall. This could have served the same purpose, giving Henry all-round protection.

The Chalice Spring and Well

Glastonbury's main supply of fresh water until the nineteenth century was the Chalice Spring, which rises on the lower slopes of the small valley formed by the Tor and Chalice hills. It provides a continuous flow of 25,000 gallons of water daily from an unknown source which is backed by sufficient thrust to send it across several miles of near sea-level moors to break ground just below the 200 ft contour. South Wales or the Mendips are areas suggested as the source. Logically, the area around the Spring had enormous potential for providing the earliest evidence of life in past millenia. It was here that the Chalice Well Trust sponsored its first excavations in 1961. The excavations were around the Wellhouse. This was built over the Spring by the Abbey authorities some time in the twelfth century to regulate the water and provide a better water supply to the Abbey, more than a hundred feet lower. Over the centuries the whole area has become buried by silt. Today the Wellhouse is called the Well.

Consistent with other sites of speculative potential, the Well excavation did not provide evidence of occupation during the critical early-Christian era. The Iron Age and Roman shards were no more than the repeated confirmation of visiting rather than staying. At a depth of

One of the glories of the 93ft by 33ft Barn is the interior roof structure which shows the incredible skill and ingenuity of medieval carpenters. The builders overcame the problem of spanning the floor area with timbers of limited length by creating a two-tier 'cruck' design, with the lower tier going from the centre of the walls half-way up the roof where they were joined by a collar. The smaller top tier stands on the collar and rises to the apex. Photographed before the museum exhibits were laid out. (*Somerset Rural Life Museum*)

twelve feet, a 2 ft 6 in long yew tree stump was found where it had obviously grown and died. Scientific examination showed it had been a living tree in Roman times, revealing that during the Roman period the ground level was about the same as the present bottom of the wellshaft, and that the water used to come out as a surface spring. Since then silt has raised the ground level. Philip Rahtz, who was the director of excavations, said that any future probe should go deep down and take in the area round the Well and a large area in the orchard above. This would establish conclusively whether there was a settlement in Christian or pre-Christian times.

The wrought iron lid covering the Chalice Well was designed by Frederick Bligh Bond, the architect and first director of excavations in the Abbey ruins after the 1907 sale. It was given as a thanks-offering for peace in 1919 by friends and lovers of Glastonbury. The symbolism in the design is based on a thirteenth-century pattern; it represents the bleeding lance and shows the visible and invisible worlds, or conscious and sub-conscious worlds, interlocked.

This pattern and theme is mirrored and magnified in the new waterfall and pools in the Chalice Well gardens. The turbulence of the pool into which the water falls represents the movement of the spring water rushing into the Chalice Well and, on a deeper level, busy consciousness.

The second circular pool with which it is intertwined respresents the stillness of the Well, the more contemplative, thoughtful life, the subconscious. The underlying concept is that in the New or Aquarian Age man will be able to make use of his latent, subconscious powers at will.

A reminder of the days when Glastonbury was famous for its waters. The Pump House built about 1750 in Magdalene Street was a product of this short-lived era, which mushroomed after an asthmatic, Matthew Chancellor of North Wootton, near Wells, had been cured by drinking some Glastonbury water on seven successive Sunday mornings in 1750. He had been told to do so in a dream concerning Glastonbury and saw some of the clearest water he had ever seen—holy water. The public reaction came to a climax the following summer; on one day there were said to be 10,000 people in the town to take the waters. It flowed from the Chalice Spring and Well which sends its clear chalybeate (impregnated with iron) water through the town. The Pump House was built over part of a culvert enclosing the spring. A list of cures including King's Evil, blindness, ulcers and deafness was published in 1751 with testimonies sworn before magistrates. The first person to have drawn attention to the Chalice Spring water was the mathematician and astrologer Dr John Dee who said he was possessed of the *elixir vitae* after drinking some in 1582. Two years earlier Dr Dee claimed he had discovered an arrangement of earthworks in Glastonbury that corresponded to the signs of the zodiac, about 350 years before Kathryn Maltwood.

4
THE NEW DIMENSIONS

Under analysis, the Glastonbury romance may seem to have lost much of its fascination, however great the scholars' desire to see the legends sustained. But parallel with these investigations, new theories were being advanced, and the old romances and traditions used as a basis for fresh research into facets one or two of the medieval monks may have suspected but would never have dared to state publicly. William of Malmesbury is thought to have dropped a big hint in this direction when, in his book on the antiquity of Glastonbury, he said of the Old Church:

> This church, then, is certainly the oldest I am acquainted with in England, and from this circumstance derives its name . . . In the pavement may be seen on every side stones designedly inlaid in triangles and squares, and figured with lead, under which, if I believe some sacred enigma to be contained, I do no injustice to religion.

Whatever William was referring to, he was not committing himself to specifics. A description was acceptable; an interpretation was not. Even in the early twentieth century, a public interpretation was not easy. Frederick Bligh Bond, the first director of excavations at the Abbey following its purchase by the Church of England, used this passage in a lecture to the Somerset Archaeological and Natural History Society in 1916. He did so in support of his thesis that Gothic architects depended on geometrical diagrams. Bond's biographer, Willian W. Kenawell, says in *The Quest at Glastonbury* that such a thesis did not find much support among scholars and churchmen, and to have spoken thus in the presence of the Society's new president, Dean (of Wells) J. Armitage Robinson, who was to act as a catalyst in Bond's life, 'was an act of foolish daring indeed'.

The Glastonbury Zodiac
The same passage has been used by Anthony Roberts in *Glastonbury: Ancient Avalon, New Jerusalem* to show how the star-like aura of the Glastonbury Zodiac lingered in Christian consciousness.

Knowledge of the Zodiac is a modern phenomenon, and it is as powerfully exciting in its raw state as are the legends at face value—and just as transient. How 'out of this world' it would be to be able to convince the world that 4,700 years ago an advanced, intelligent people laid out on the earth's surface in and around Glastonbury a zodiac with twelve effigies, all conforming to the familiar constellations in the heavens, and known as the signs of the zodiac. For thousands of years it bore silent witness to the heavens it reflected until an astute and beautiful woman' Kathryn Maltwood, metaphorically brought it down to earth.

The Zodiac, ten miles in diameter and thirty in circumference, is a part of esoteric Glastonbury, where more tensile insight sets its adherents apart: people who see not only the wonders of the past, but a vision of the coming of the Aquarian Age or the Christian Second Coming. There is an equal and opposite orthodox school of thought, too, and so far as the Zodiac claim is concerned, they regard it as interesting, but rubbish. They cannot understand how the boundaries of these 4,700-year-old effigies were chosen, conforming to lines of rivers, rhynes (moor ditches), hedgerows, roadways, paths, hills, earthworks, when some of these things are known to have been shaped only within the past 300 years. Even the claim that the figures can be easily detected from the air has not convinced the sceptics.

Those who believe in the Zodiac's existence say it can best be seen from the air. Kathryn Maltwood discovered the outline of Leo, in part represented by the course of the River Cary near Somerton, in the mid-1920s. She found the other effigies within a ten-mile radius of Butleigh. Their boundaries are delineated by lanes, ditches, streams, embankments and roads. Testing the Zodiac, Mrs Maltwood found that a planisphere placed over the figures drawn on a scale map corresponded exactly. Most easily identifiable of the figures is Pisces, the fish, represented by Wearyall Hill; the Tor is part of the Aquarius effigy, which doubles as the Phoenix. The photograph shows the dove representing Libra, which lies between Baltonsborough and Barton St David. *(Grael Publications)*

28

Kathryn Maltwood discovered the Zodiac in the 1920s during a time when she was illustrating *The High History of the Holy Grail*, a Norman-French manuscript written about 1225.

When deep in the text of the book, she realised that there was a relationship between the ground plan it described in and around Glastonbury and the ancient constellation zodiac in the heavens. The author stated in the book that his tale was taken from Glastonbury Abbey. While

Famous for its medieval panelled facade, the George & Pilgrims Hotel was rebuilt by Abbot Selwood (1457-93) as an inn for wealthy pilgrims to the Abbey. The majority of the panelled compartments are pierced and glazed; others, not needed for windows, are filled in with solid masonry.

Mrs Maltwood was illustrating the Arthurian Grail quest in the *High History* she read of an encounter with a lion at Somerton. Looking at the Ordnance Survey map, she realised the course of the River Cary was like the outline of the underside of a lion. She looked for and found the rest of the effigy. Others followed, all combining myth, legend and place-names. After more research came her books: *Glastonbury's Temple of the Stars* and *Enchantments of Britain*.

The Glastonbury Zodiac, said Mrs Maltwood, was the biggest of all Britain's antiquities—some of the effigies were up to five miles long.

In *Glastonbury: Ancient Avalon, New Jerusalem* author John Michell, deprecating the way past academics had likened Ancient Britons to painted savages, writes:

Academics would have had us believe that during this period, Britain was peopled only by painted savages. Yet these people left us such geometrically perfect, astronomically orientated instruments of their complex earth science as at the Stonehenge and Callanish stone circles, the ley line phenomenon and the enormous star charts called zodiac temples. Research in the past two decades has shown that the ancient Britons were far more knowledgeable in astronomy than was at first thought. The megalithic stone monuments, almost all that is left of their ancient times, on analysis have shown achievements in astronomical knowledge in these islands unsurpassed by anyone in history.

If Mrs Maltwood and Mr Edwards (discoverer of a zodiac in South Wales) had had access to this new evidence, they too may have concluded that the zodiac temple builders needed to borrow from no one in this science; their own ancient traditions, steeped in star lore and star science, were guidelines by which the temples were constructed.

The whole subject of the Temple of the Stars is vastly complex and riddled with enchanting coincidences. Those seeking for understanding and enlightenment find stories from Celtic mythology come thundering through to make sense of other isolated stories, fables, place-names, geographical features, alignments, all taking the Zodiac concept towards wider acceptance and deeper philosophical and metaphysical meanings. And as the heavens move from one constellation to another this Zodiac shows the present time to be on the threshold of Aquarius—the rising phoenix of the New Age, the effigy that covers Glastonbury Tor.

The Riddles of the Tor

The Abbey is the heart of the pilgrim's Glastonbury; the Tor is its beacon or landmark. Visible above the moors for long distances, its conical form spirals into the sky, crowned by the old church tower.

In tune with the general spiritual mysticism of Glastonbury, the Tor has its own riddles: it is said to be man-made, hollow, the place where the people living in the area anciently were buried, the mythological entrance to the Underworld and, more recently, the site of a religious maze, 3,000 years old and similar to the Cretan maze.

The theories of hollowness, a burial place or the entrance to the Underworld have yet to be fully put to the test. The man-made concept failed the test. During the 1964-66 excavations on the summit, the fact of finding hard rock, known as Tor Burrs, underneath the summit turf showed it to be a natural hill. Philip Rahtz in his excavation report states that the first 200 feet are of middle lias clays and limestones, the middle slopes are of middle-upper lias clays and limestones, and the summit consists of Midford sand deposits, consolidated into dense masses known as Tor Burrs. The hardness of this capping has helped resist erosion of the middle-upper lias deposits and is responsible for the steepness and isolation of the Tor.

The Glastonbury Maze

Coming to the maze, its outward signs are the various terraces, more visible on the Tor's northern, or town, side. The maze theory has been advanced by Geoffrey Russell of Glanmire, County Cork, Eire, who has researched hard, and assiduously argued its possibility.

He had not taken any interest in the Tor before retiring as chairman of two investment trust companies in County Cork, but he was well acquainted with the Grail literature and Arthurian stories. Being interested in the maze as a world phenomenon, he suspected a link with the Grail story, possibly in Glastonbury. The Tor was that link.

He studied photographs of the Tor's terraces, and became convinced that the Tor was entirely shaped by man—probably about 3,000 years ago. The purpose of a maze or labyrinth was as a path for penitents to use to reach some form of

The Tor's northern face showing the terraces that led Geoffery Russell to believe the entire surface of the hill was landscaped by prehistoric man in the form of a three-dimensional circular maze. The aerial photograph shows the Tor against the background of the Vale of Avalon and the Mendip Hills. The terraces are clearly seen Several years ago a photogrammetric survey was made of the Tor (some of the money for the work coming from the Maltwood bequest). Geoffrey Russell said that the photographs showed that the lower four terraces or paths had not been greatly eroded by time.

In Celtic mythology the land of the dead was known as Avalon and was always a hill surrounded by water, the supposed prehistoric condition of the Vale of Avalon. Bligh Bond called the Tor a 'hill of vision'. Geoffrey Russell, and others, believe it was the legendary *Caer Sidi* of the Welsh bards—one of the three great labours of the Britons and the centre of initiation into the Celtic mysteries in honour of the goddess Ceridwen.

On a more mundane plane, others ascribe the terraces to agricultural workings, such as vineyards or strip-lynchets. The accepted geological opinion is that the terraces are the natural result of the erosion of strata of varying hardness. (*Photograph of northern side of Tor by Brian Walker; aerial photograph by courtesy the Pendragon Society, Bristol*)

(below)
The distant Tor Hill and St Michael's tower silhouetted in the waters of the Abbot's Fish Pond in the Abbey grounds, south of the old monastic buildings. The Pond is fed by water from the Chalice Spring on its way to the Pump House, and on to the moors and the sea. American scientist Donald L. Cyr, writing in *Glastonbury: Ancient Avalon, New Jerusalem* suggests that treasurers from the Abbey are buried in the Pond.

purification. Its early meaning throughout the world was to represent the symbol of God and the path to the soul of God. Geoffrey Russell believed that the end of the Quest of the Grail was Christ.

Similar to the Cretan labyrinth, the Tor has seven inter-communicating but not overlapping pathways. The Cretan one was said to be an imitation of an earlier Egyptian one. Other prehistoric monuments with seven stages were the Hindu mountain Meru and the Hebrew Tower of Babel. Nearer home, a 3,500-year-old maze carving exists at Tintagel, supposed birthplace of the legendary Arthur, and the symbol is also in the Hollywood Stone discovered in the Wicklow Mountains in Ireland.

Philip Rahtz has given encouragement to Geoffrey Russell in his pursuit to find evidence to prove his theory, and said in his Tor excavations report: 'If the maze theory were demonstrated to be true, it would clearly be of the greatest relevance to the origins of Glastonbury as a religious centre.' Geoffrey Russell believes such an engineering feat would place the maze in the same league as Stonehenge, and having established an early pagan religious centre at Glastonbury, it would give fresh backing to the area's importance in early Christian times.

Ley Lines

Glastonbury features in two of the country's major ley lines. One is between Glastonbury

The surrounds of St Benedict's Church, about 300 yards west of the Abbey, were, in 1607, the high water mark for a vast flood that reached across the moors from the Bristol Channel fourteen miles away. This was one of the effects of the breakdown of the drainage systems on the moors caused by the disappearance of the monks about seventy years earlier.

But it is to the penultimate abbot, Abbot Bere, that St Benedict's owes its greatest debt. He carried out a big restoration and built the north aisle and possibly the tower. The first church on this site may have been consecrated as early as 1100AD. Until the mid-seventeenth century the dedication of the church was to St Benignus, said to be a disciple of St Patrick.

Abbey, Stonehenge and Canterbury Cathedral, and the other runs from St Michael's Mount (off the south Cornish coast) through St Michael's Church on the Tor summit and on to ancient Avebury circle or temple in Wiltshire.

Ley lines are part of the new twentieth-century knowledge of prehistoric science. They arise from perfect alignments of ancient sites: megalithic stones, tumuli, barrows, camps, crosses, churches built on pre-Christian sites and holy wells. Straight lines drawn to connect these features are known as ley lines. Their exact purpose is unknown, but they are uncannily accurate. The one from St Michael's Mount to the Tor and Avebury also takes in other churches dedicated to St Michael and St George. John

A. Creed tested the 150-mile line from the Abbey to Canterbury Cathedral via Stonehenge for his book *Glastonbury Tales*. Using a piece of cotton across one-inch-to-the-mile Ordnance Survey maps he found it accurate to a twentieth of an inch of the centre of Stonehenge. He conceded that the error was his and not the designers!

The entire countryside is covered with multitudes of ley lines, and these two are not the only ones involving Glastonbury.

Farmer's son Alfred Watkins, who discovered and named ley lines, was a Herefordshire merchant. He suggested ancient man used them for navigation across the deserts and forests between isolated communities. Simplifying the method, it used the same principles as two or more people travelling along a compass bearing during the night—one person walks along the correct bearing until almost out of sight, and then the others catch up, and so on until the objective is reached. With the ley lines, mounds, stone pillars and cairns were raised at the 'catch-up' points, but on a much larger scale. This over-simplification of the ley line principle no more than touches the surface. The intention here is merely to show how Glastonbury fits in among the giants of a religious phenomenon that has physical attributes that are logical but yet inexplicable.

5

THE LURE OF THE LEGENDS

On the lower slopes of the Tor in the darkness of a summer evening, a crowd stands in a circle behind a rope laid on the ground. To pass over is forbidden. Unseen and unheard several men and women, in ceremonial red and black robes, stand in set positions in the centre of the rope circle. They have reached the climax of their ritual. It is a moment when the powers of heaven are connected with the powers on earth.

Assisting this momentary connection with a heavenly host are latter-day Essenes. Each year at true midnight (1.00 am BST) on the longest day (21 June) they are in the top corner of a field on the Tor's eastern slopes.

The Essenes

The Essenes believe that Glastonbury is the world's most important power point, where solar and terrestial forces meet. At this particular climatic moment of silence angels who have been guarding our planet for the past year are leaving. In the few seconds as the new ones arrive and take up their duties at other cosmic points, the earth 'fort' is held by these Essenes. Once it is all over the Essenes process, with admirable dignity for 1.00 am in a Somerset field, to their coach waiting to return to the Town Hall. There they meet and share their food with members of the

The respect shown by the Brotherhood of the Essenes for animal life, and dogs in particular, can be seen by the prominence given to these paintings during the annual ceremony in Glastonbury Town Hall. Held late at night, it precedes the mystic ritual on the Tor slopes. During these ceremonies Essene speakers normally emphasise the role of animals—deliberately without means of speech, they believe—to test the human race on matters of kindness and consideration. The idea of Christ, at his second coming, appearing with a dog beside him is not foreign to Essenes, by conviction vegetarians. (*Brian Walker*)

Druids ascend the Tor for the Spring Festival of Beltane to hold a Gorsedd and Eisteddfod on the summit. These are members of the Order of Bards, Ovates and Druids and the sword Excalibur is being carried in front of their former Chosen Chief, the late Ross Nichols. The Order believe that there was once a Druidic University at Glastonbury, and that if there is anywhere in England an area of supernatural, visionary land, it is at Glastonbury. In a Cornish version of the Glastonbury legends, Jesus was said to have studied at this university to prepare for his ministry, because he found the people thought the same way as he did. William Blake, the mystic and poet who wrote 'Jerusalem' which is sometimes referred to as England's second national anthem and is believed to allude to Christ at Glastonbury, was apparently a Chosen Chief of the Order of Druids for many years. (*Brian Walker*)

public, before getting back into the coach and driving off into the night towards London.

The Brotherhood of the Essenes are a closed order of initiates guided by a woman, known as The Centre. They claim to be a restoration of the Essenes in Palestine at the time of Christ and to be performing exactly the same task—preparing the way for the coming of Christ, but this time the Second Coming—at Glastonbury. The annual visits to Glastonbury have been going on for more than fifty years—and there is no indication when they are likely to stop.

There are many groups and individuals who, like the Essenes, find Glastonbury a high-powered spiritual centre, irrespective of the functional impotence of the once-great Abbey for the last 440 years. To them Glastonbury is alive, if not beckoning.

Geoffrey Ashe

It beckoned writer Geoffrey Ashe while he was working in Toronto in 1955. Something innocuous and now forgotten recalled Glastonbury to his mind, and he went to the city library to find out more about the town. In one book he read of a prophecy attributed to a former Glastonbury monk, Austin Ringwode, saying: 'The abbey will one day be repaired and rebuilt for the like worship which has ceased; and then peace and plenty for a long time will abound'. 'The words hit me with the force of a revelation,' wrote Geoffrey Ashe twenty-three years later in his book *Miracles*. This was not because of any faith in such prophecies, but because the words were apt to him personally. 'They gave me my marching orders.'

From that moment, he recalled, his serious career as a writer, indeed the whole structure of his effective life changed. Glastonbury was going to be reborn, and that was what he had to work for by using his only talent, writing.

He returned to England and two years later his popular seller, *King Arthur's Avalon*, appeared. Since then many more books on Glastonbury and Arthur have been published. Behind him now are his years as a consultant with the Ford Motor Company and a lecturer at the Polytechnic in London, only writing in his spare time. He is now an Arthurian consultant in his own right, in demand by tour operators from the United States and Canada, where he also lectures on Arthur and the mysteries of Britain.

Ironically, the words that set off this change were probably mere invention. Having never come across them again in his researches, Geoffrey Ashe queried the book's author, Christopher Hollis, the historian. What he was

Even in private hands the Abbey ruins were a centre for pilgrimage, celebration and thanksgiving. This 1854 drawing shows a procession through the ruins to mark the opening of the Central Somerset Railway in the town. The impact of such an event can be seen by the banners: 'Railways and Civilisation' and 'Where There's a Will, There's a Way'.

In 1897 there was a famous procession of clergy through the ruins. As they filed along they sang 'The Church's One Foundation'. According to one account: 'The listeners noticed there was a kind of *concordia discors* and when the leaders of the straggling line had finished one verse of the hymn, others were halfway on. Still the procession forged ahead, and still old echoes sent back the strain of enthusiasm, independent of the single conductor's baton.'

told took him back to a nineteenth-century magazine article, but no further. But the historian did admit that Ringwode was a suspect character: there had been no record of any monk at the Abbey with that name. Did Geoffrey Ashe feel duped? No, Toronto to him was a directional push, and a big one. He had never had a moment's doubt that the commitment was correct. He feels he is on the right track, but he is still not absolutely certain what that track is.

His experience over the bogus prophecy is characteristic of the way the Glastonbury imp treats its devotees. For some it is heartbreaking, and the devotion usually starts with such fine ennobling intentions.

Miracles at Glastonbury have been performing since 1970. This is the name of a company who present original and adapted medieval-style miracle plays in the evocative atmosphere of the Abbey ruins—on fine days against a background of the setting sun. The plays run for a six-week season, normally from the last week in June until the first in August. The founder and director of Miracles at Glastonbury, Kenneth Janes, is a native of the town, and is the drama professor at Barnard College, Columbia University, New York City. Many of Kenneth Janes' own students have been able to participate in the plays through scholarship awards from the Richard Rogers Fund. (*Brian Walker*)

Rutland Boughton

Composer Rutland Boughton conceived Glastonbury as a form of English Bayreuth, a centre for annual national musical festivals, incorporating dramas based on the Arthurian legends. He was a man of considerable talent and extreme national popularity, his fame being second only to Sir Edward Elgar. A countrywide appeal for funds to build a National Theatre of Music and Drama at Glastonbury was launched in 1913. Signatories to the appeal included Sir Thomas Beecham, Sir Edward Elgar, John Galsworthy, George Bernard Shaw and Sir Henry Wood. This worthy dream evaporated with the First World War, but a Glastonbury Festival of Music, Dance and Mystic Drama was held about 1921 in the town's Assembly Rooms. It included the first performance of Boughton's *The Immortal Hour*, which later had a run of more than 500 performances in London.

Boughton was a committed communist and detested the personality cult that surrounded him; a wise personal philosophy, for it was his personality that lost him whatever chance of success he had with his festivals. His political ideals caused a final split with the festival directors in 1926 over the nativity play *Bethlehem*.

A model reconstruction of Glastonbury Abbey, circa 1539, viewed from the north-west, on display in the Abbey. It is the work of Nicholas Gaffney and the result of more than 5,000 hours of patient work. The scale used was a sixteenth of an inch to one foot.

He had wanted, for a London performance, Christ to be born in a miner's cottage and Herod to be cast as a cigar-smoking capitalist, supported by the army and police. Boughton's disaffection with the local population was caused by his private life, which scàndalised townspeople sufficiently for them to withdraw their children from his School of Music and Drama. Some of those children of fifty years ago now remember his eccentric musical genius with warm affection, but his festival project, which had attracted top performers, faded into oblivion.

Kathryn Maltwood

Kathryn Maltwood, daughter of a judge, member of the intellectual and influential Bloomsbury Circle, discovered the Zodiac not long after Rutland Boughton's departure. This has a 'heaven on earth' theme—something that recurs like a gravitational pull among so many of the people attracted to Glastonbury with inspired ideas. The star patterns in the sky were reflected on the gound so that those who walked within the Zodiac also walked in heaven. But it was, according to one commentator on her notes and papers, a perpetual disappointment to her that she never received academic recogni-

tion. She left a bequest to the Royal Society of Arts, of which she had been a member, of £100,000 for the furtherance of archaeological research in Somerset. None of this has yet been used to give the Zodiac a greater chance of credibility on the grounds that it would be an archaeological impossibility. There is no accepted archaeological basis for the Zodiac. Since Mrs Maltwood's revelations at Glastonbury, others have been discovered at Kingston upon Thames in Surrey, Pumpsaint and Prescelly in South Wales, and Durham.

Bligh Bond

Frederick Bligh Bond, first director of excavations at Glastonbury Abbey after it came into the hands of the Church of England, stunned the archaeological and ecclesiastical world ten years after operations began. He published a book revealing that he had been receiving messages from a former abbey monk, by means of automatic writing, as a guide to the correct sites to excavate, and much of what he was given had considerably helped his work.

The son of a clergyman, he was a practising architect in Bristol when he was chosen to lead the excavation. A year later, in 1909, he was appointed architect to the Bath and Wells Diocese, an honorary position. What his high-principled masters did not know about the eccentric Bligh Bond was that within months of the Anglican purchase of the abbey in 1907, he was in touch with its former residents, in the afterworld.

Describing the first contact, in Bond's Bristol office, with a Captain John Bartlett as medium, Bond's biographer, William W. Kenawell, wrote that the reply from the other side to his initial question 'set Bond's heart afire in a search that in the end was to destroy him'. Bond was sacked as director of excavations in 1922 for refusing to work with a co-director appointed by the Somerset Archaeological Society. Of course, this was merely a formal reason. The basic ones, Kenawall says, 'were too numerous and too personal to be admitted by a learned Society'.

Apart from the obvious anathema felt by church and scholar over the automatic writing, Bond had other troubles. Firstly, his wife, whom he left after four years of marriage, spent the next quarter of a century pursuing him with a venomous whispering campaign, the National Vigilance Campaign and private inquiry agents. Secondly, he clashed with the diocesan heirarchy when his appointment as diocesan architect ended in 1913, which he first discovered when he saw a newspaper advertisement offering the post. Thirdly, he clashed over his successor by

The Abbey was first acquired by the Austin family in 1862. Mr Stanley Austin (*centre*) who inherited the estate from his father announced his intention to sell eight months before the auction. To try and secure it for the Church of England, the Bishop of Bath and Wells, Dr George Kennion, spent the intervening months writing to various people privately asking for guarantees of subscriptions. By auction day, 6 June 1907, about £15,000 had been guaranteed. No formal agreement had been negotiated between the purchaser—politician and manufacturer Ernest Jardine (*right*)—and the church before the auction, but he had stated his intention to hand it over to the church at the same price he paid which was £30,000. Two days after the sale the Bishop wrote: 'It seemed to me that it would be a matter of very deep regret to many members of the Church of England if the Abbey were to pass into the possession of any other Communion'. On the left of the picture is the auctioneer, Mr R. Bowring.

making a professional protest about the appointment to the Royal Institute of British Architects' Standing Committee on Practice.

Finally, he clashed with the scholars by establishing 666ft as the true length of the Abbey, it being part of an ancient geometric formula, and over the importance he attached to his belief that the Edgar Chapel wall ended in an apse rather than a straight wall.

Bligh Bond had a childlike emotional intensity, which too often showed in its raw state, and a possessive infatuation with Glastonbury Abbey which in the end consumed him. But he did not let his monkish friends, known as the Brotherhood of Watchers or the Company of Avalon, so possess his professional life that it was inept. His attempts to get recognition for geometric formulae in building construction, particularly Gothic architecture, was in a sense pioneering work. Today many others are working along the same lines, taking it back as far as Stonehenge, and adding a new dimension and understanding to the 'ancient wisdom'.

The 1907 Sale of the Abbey

The Church of England acquired the Abbey for £30,000 at a public auction on 6 June, 1907, the ruins having been in private hands for about 370 years. The auction, in the Abbey grounds,

The Abbey Gateway adjoining, on the left, the Gatehouse which contains a museum. At the time of the sale of the Abbey the numbers of visitors had been increasing each year. In 1903 there were 6,482 visitors and this had risen to 9,970 for 1906, the year before the auction. Seventy years later (1976) there were 142,000 visitors and the number is still increasing. The Abbey's running costs are about £30,000 a year.

was a magnificent affair with a large marquee, an impressive sale brochure and the presence of many of the most important people in the country. The result was to some extent a foregone conclusion, for the Church of England had made no secret of its intention to buy. The Bishop of Bath and Wells, Dr George Kennion, had launched a private purchase fund in the hope of raising enough money to secure the property. By 6 June the fund had reached about £15,000 and the remaining cash for the sale to go through was guaranteed by Mr Ernest Jardine, a lace-machine manufacturer from Nottingham and at that time the prospective Unionist candidate for East Somerset.

It was, possibly, a close shave for the Anglicans. As the bidding was proceeding, a woman of Spanish-American descent was on her way, intent on buying the Abbey. By a strange quirk of fate she had been delayed on her journey. It is thought she missed a rail connection at Ever-

Each summer Anglicans and Roman Catholics hold separate pilgrimages to Glastonbury involving processions through the streets by thousands of people. The Anglican pilgrimage, held on the last Saturday in June, is centred on the Abbey ruins. The first events start early in the morning and the climax is the Evensong, which is preceded by a colourful procession of clergy in their capes and priestly vestments from St John's Church, down the High Street, and into the Abbey. In recent years the number of pilgrims has averaged between 6,000 and 7,000. These pilgrimages have been held annually since 1924, apart from the Second World War years. They originated from a visit by the Guild of Servants of the Sanctuary which received permission to sing its office in the ruins in the early 1920s. (*Brian Walker*)

Some of the thousands who attend Anglican pilgrimages sitting on the grass under the mid-day sun during the service of Holy Eucharist. (*Brian Walker*)

The Roman Catholics sometimes start their pilgrimage on the lower slopes of the Tor and process to the Convent Field behind their church in Magdalene Street, the pilgrims carrying life-size crosses. In 1965 there were about 20,000 pilgrims for the historic visit to the Abbey. The large crowd saw the then Apostolic Delegate, Archbishop Igino Cardinale, place a crown of gold on the statue of Our Lady of Glastonbury. (*Brian Walker*)

Our Lady of Glastonbury in the Roman Catholic Church in Magdalene Street. (*Norman Heal*)

creech or was misdirected there. She arrived when the bidding had closed. What happened next, according to information given by Major Wellesley Tudor Pole in an interview before his death, was that she approached the buyer and immediately either made an offer £5,000 in excess of the £30,000 or asked if he would accept a profit of £5,000. The proposition was rejected. A higher figure was offered, and again rejected. Major Tudor Pole, who was present at the auction and at whose Bristol home the woman had spent the previous night as a guest, said that she did not disclose who she was bidding for. It has been supposed that she intended to buy the Abbey and present it to the English Roman Catholic Benedictines, who were possibly totally unaware of her efforts.

Roman Catholic Pilgrimages

At that time the Roman Catholics owned the Chalice Well property at the foot of Glastonbury Tor where they had a chapel and noviciate. This had been founded by the Sacred Heart Fathers in 1888. Their main devotion to Glastonbury is based on the belief that the Old Church of wattles was the earliest dedication to the Virgin Mary north of the Alps. Like the Anglicans, they have their own pilgrimages at Glastonbury each summer. About 20,000 Catholics took part in the 1965 pilgrimage, which was held in the Abbey, where mass was said publicly for the first time since the Dissolution. The Apostolic Delegate Archbishop Igino Cardinale marked the special occasion by placing a golden crown on the head of the statue of 'Our Lady of Glastonbury'. Their pilgrimage was held at the Abbey the following year, but they have now returned to the field at the back of the Convent as the main pilgrimage gathering place.

Major Wellesley Tudor Pole

Major Tudor Pole was another of the talented visionaries attracted to Glastonbury. He first visited the town in 1905 and two years later he spent a weekend at the Roman Catholic College at Chalice Well. Afterwards he predicted he would one day own the Well. This came true in 1958, when he set up the Chalice Well Trust with some friends to buy the property which was then a school. The owner, after the Noviciate had closed, was the poetess Miss Alice Buckton, who wrote the play *Eager Heart*.

Major Tudor Pole's purpose in acquiring the Well property, and that of the trustees, was to preserve and safeguard it for perpetuity. He firmly believed that from Glastonbury would go a message essential for the New Age.

His attachment to the Chalice Well flowed from his belief that at this spot the veil between heaven and earth was thin. Such spots are nearly always associated with a healing spring or well, and with holy persons from the past. Chalice Well fits both conditions. By preserving these places peacefully Tudor Pole believed pilgrims could not only find rest, but their inner perceptions would be stimulated and brought out into the open. He personally revered Chalice Well as the first gateway in Britain through which Christ's message entered. The Trust's purpose was to keep the atmosphere 'peaceful, beautiful and worthy' to be used once again as a gateway for a message for the Coming Times.

Tudor Pole played a significant role in the spiritual life of the nation during the Second World War. He founded the Big Ben Silent Minute, when people prayed silently for peace during the minute that it took Big Ben to sound 9.00 pm. This was the reason Big Ben was restored to the airwaves. It had been removed and replaced by the Greenwich time signal because it had been felt that Big Ben pin-pointed London. Having failed to persuade the BBC to change its policy, Tudor Pole took his problem to Churchill. The wartime leader's imagination was fired and he rang up the Director-General of the BBC on the spot, in Tudor Pole's presence. The result was that Big Ben was back on the air on 11 November, 1940.

That 'Indefinable Something'

Many people feel sufficiently drawn to Glastonbury to move into the town, to be close to the indefinable something that satisfies their soul more than at any other place on earth. Others make temporary contact as pilgrims, either individually or collectively. And the townspeople live placidly through it all, appreciating the legends, accepting the outsiders' sensibilities, but to a large extent unexcited and unmoved.

They have grown sceptical over the years of bright ideas and elixirs, and some believe they are being preserved and protected for some future event. Former Mayor Miss Edith Rice, who has participated in many of the activities introduced to the town by the outsiders, has found them enriching. But she advised that it was necessary to be open-minded to the new ideas. Geoffrey Ashe said that one of the stumbling blocks for a few outsiders was that they arrived with some kind of a package deal,

Believed to be the first permanent cross in the Abbey grounds since the Dissolution, the wood was a gift from the Queen, from an oak tree growing on Duchy of Cornwall land. It was dedicated by the then Bishop of Bath and Wells, Dr Edward Henderson, in 1965.

Glastonbury's Tor Fair is one of the oldest in the country. Permission to hold it was originally granted by Henry I in 1127 to Abbot Robert of Winchester. It was first held on the Tor and lasted at least two days. In the eighteenth century it also had the name of Colt Fair because of the vast numbers of colts, especially sucklings, brought for sale. Today sheep are the main animal merchandise for sale on Tor Fair Day, the second Monday in September. The scene in this picture has passed into history for the sheep sale was switched to the town's cattle market in George Street in 1977. The present Fair Field is sandwiched between Benedict Street and Street Road. Tor Fair's funfair activities continue until the end of the week. (*Brian Walker*)

believing they knew what should happen in Glastonbury. In his twenty-four years of contact with the town he has changed the emphasis of his own ideas considerably. To him Joseph of Arimathea and Arthur do not really matter a great deal. They are symptoms that have grown out of the Glastonbury mystique.

Expert on Arthurian affairs that he is, to Geoffrey Ashe Arthur has been but a sideline, not affecting the sense of mission that hit him so forcibly in Toronto. It has sharpened his sensi-

bilities, and helped him to mark time. (He was secretary and co-founder of the Camelot Research Committee that organised the five seasons of excavations at South Cadbury from 1966–1970).

He firmly believes that there is more to come at Glastonbury, something indefinable, of which he has but a faint suspicion. 'Something is going to happend here, maybe soon, maybe not. I do not know. I cannot force it, but it will be enormously important and make a tremendous difference,' he says with absolute calmness and sincerity.

He is not alone. From the medieval belief in the return of Arthur, shared by many even today, to the Essenes, Wellesley Tudor Pole, the Zodiac's pointer to the Aquarian Age, and the sleeping, expectant town, there is a visible stirring.

Is this some British Lorelei beckoning Utopians to destruction, or a crescendo of prophetic impulses in tune with Blake's vision: of building Jerusalem in England's green and pleasant land?

INDEX

ACKNOWLEDGEMENTS

The co-operation and assistance of many people have contributed a large part to the information and photographs in this book. In particular, thanks are extended to Philip Rahtz, Peter Poyntz-Wright, John Simmons, Pam Haydon and Brian Walker.